CW00369404

healthy
recipes

DELICIOUS, HEALTHY RECIPES
FROM AROUND THE WORLD

HELEN ADAMS

This is a Parragon Book
First published in 2004

Parragon
Queen Street House
4 Queen Street
Bath BA1 1HE

Created and produced by The Bridgewater Book Company Ltd.

ISBN: 1-40543-156-3

Printed in China

NOTE

*This book uses metric and imperial measurements. Follow the same units of
measurement throughout; do not mix metric and imperial. All spoon measurements
are level: teaspoons are assumed to be 5 ml and tablespoons are assumed to be 15 ml.
Unless otherwise stated, milk is assumed to be full fat, eggs and individual vegetables
such as potatoes are medium, and pepper is freshly ground black pepper.*

*Ovens should be preheated to the specified temperature. If using a fan-assisted oven,
check the manufacturer's instructions for adjusting the time and temperature.*

*Recipes using raw or very lightly cooked eggs should be avoided by infants, the elderly,
pregnant women, convalescents and anyone suffering from an illness. Pregnant and
breastfeeding women are advised to avoid eating peanuts and peanut products.*

Contents

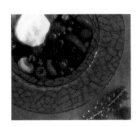

Introduction

Many of us have taken on board the message that what we eat impacts significantly on our health. However, it is easy to become bewildered by the complexities and contradictions in the advice on different foods and dietary regimes that we now face on a daily basis. This book offers a refreshing and inspirational approach to healthy eating based on sound nutritional

principles and offers a range of easy-to-prepare yet imaginative recipes. The exciting flavours and textures in all these dishes will serve as an antidote to the perceived view that a healthy diet is rather restrictive. This is food that you can really enjoy while improving your health and wellbeing at the same time.

Healthy Eating Guidelines

In order for your body to maintain itself in good working order, it needs to have a regular and balanced supply of nutrients. This means making the right choice of foods, and nutritionists have developed a way of helping us without having to grapple with detailed nutritional data. They have identified the basic food types and divided them

into five separate groups. These groups are shown here, with the group we need the most listed first, reducing to those we need least listed last.

Breads, Cereals, Pasta, Noodles, Rice and Potatoes

These foods are rich in carbohydrates, which provide the body with energy, and are low in fat. They contain B vitamins, selenium, calcium and iron as well as fibre. Up to one-third of your daily food intake should be chosen from this group.

Vegetables and Fruits

These nutritious foods are rich in vitamins, particularly A, C and E, known as antioxidants, and minerals such as calcium, potassium, magnesium and iron. They are extremely good sources of fibre and are also virtually fat-free. You can eat as many as you like of these, and most health organizations recommend eating

at least five portions of vegetables and fruits in total a day.

Meat, Poultry, Fish, Beans, Nuts, Seeds and Eggs

These foods are our main source of protein, essential for maintaining the body's functions. Meat, poultry and fish are rich in B vitamins and minerals such as iron, zinc and magnesium, but they also contain varying amounts of saturated and unsaturated fat.

Milk, Cheese and Yogurt

Dairy foods offer good sources of calcium, provide protein and also contain the vitamins A, D and B6 (riboflavin). However, they are also high in saturated fats, so your consumption needs to be limited. When buying foods from this group, try to choose lower-fat varieties to help in this way.

Fats and Sugars

These foods are essential to a healthy diet but they are only needed in small quantities. It is preferable to eat more unsaturated fats than saturated fats. Unsaturated fats are found in olive oil and other vegetable oils, oily fish and fish oils, butter, avocados, nuts and seeds.

Healthy Ingredients and Options

While the carbohydrate-rich foods are the mainstay of a healthy diet, we need to be wary of falling into the trap of eating them with saturated fats and sugars – for instance, breakfast cereals with sugar and milk, pasta with creamy sauces, bread spread with butter and jam, or potatoes in the form of chips, deep-fried in oil. There are many other ways to enjoy carbohydrates without counteracting their beneficial effects. For extra benefits, opting for wholemeal or wholegrain varieties of bread, rice, pasta and breakfast cereals will maximize your intake of dietary fibre and vitamins.

Variety is the key to getting the most from vegetables and fruits in your diet, in terms of both the different nutrients they have and their fibre content, in addition to taste and texture. Bananas, for instance, are rich in potassium, which can help to regulate blood pressure, and citrus fruits are high in fibre and vitamin C.

Spinach, carrots and peppers offer betacarotene, which the body converts into vitamin A. Some studies have found that lycopene, which gives tomatoes their bright red colouring, can help to reduce the risk of prostate cancer in men, and possibly cervical cancer in women. It appears that canned or other types of processed tomatoes are even more beneficial than the fresh variety.

You can avoid loss of vitamins from vegetables and fruits by taking a few simple steps in their preparation. Avoid peeling them where possible, avoid letting them stand in water before cooking, and avoid overcooking them.

Your choice of protein source has an important part to play in maintaining a healthy diet. Skinless turkey and chicken are relatively low in fat, particularly saturated fats, although the brown meat is fattier than the white. Lean cuts of pork are surprisingly low in fat – more so than beef or lamb. While white fish is low in fat, oily fish such as salmon, tuna, mackerel, herrings, sardines and anchovies contains omega-3 fatty

acids, which are thought to be protective against heart disease and strokes, and may be helpful for those suffering from arthritis. Tofu is a particularly healthy protein source: it is low in saturated fat and cholesterol and contains protective antioxidants. Dried beans, peas and lentils are another good, low-fat source of protein, but they are best served with wholegrain rice and plant foods to provide the correct balance of nutrients. Nuts are high in fat, but it is mostly of the unsaturated kind which, rather than raising blood cholesterol levels, may even help to reduce them. Hazelnuts, walnuts and almonds are good choices.

Fatty foods are seductive because the fats and oils they contain are phenomenal flavour-boosters. However, other healthier ingredients can be used in place of fats to contribute to the taste of dishes, such as herbs, including garlic and fresh root ginger, spices, tomato purée, olives, capers, reduced-salt soy sauce, Worcestershire sauce, Tabasco sauce, stock, vegetable and fruit juices and wine.

Healthy Cooking Methods

Once you have chosen the right foods for a healthy, balanced diet, it is vital to follow through with a healthy approach to cooking them. Steaming requires no additional fat and retains all the nutrients and flavour, while grilling, barbecuing or griddling (using a dry cast-iron or aluminium ridged grill pan on the hob) seals in all the flavour with little or no need for fat. Microwaving is also a fat-free cooking method. Rapidly stir-frying foods in a preheated wok with a minimal amount of oil is also a relatively healthy cooking method, and again maximizes the taste and texture of ingredients.

Using a large, heavy-based, non-stick frying pan, you can dry-fry fresh lean mince or bacon, thereby releasing its own fat, which can then be drained away. Use a proprietary oil spray for shallow-frying, or alternatively, try 'sautéeing' vegetables without any additional fat in a covered frying pan or saucepan, where they will cook in their own juices.

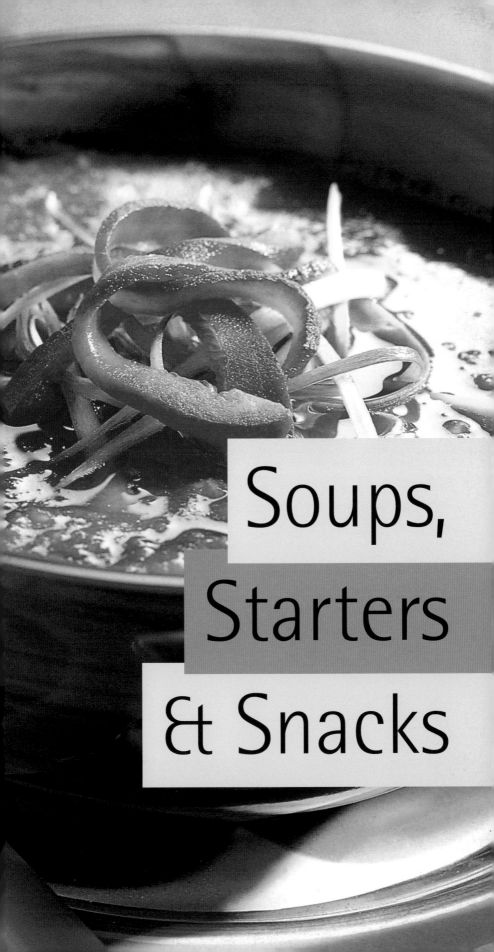

Soups, Starters & Snacks

Tomato &
Red Pepper Soup

Sweet red peppers and tangy tomatoes are blended together in a smooth
vegetable soup that makes a perfect starter or light lunch.

serves 4

2 large red peppers

1 large onion, chopped

2 celery sticks, chopped

1 garlic clove, crushed

600 ml/1 pint vegetable stock

2 bay leaves

800 g/1 lb 12 oz canned plum tomatoes

salt and pepper

2 spring onions, finely shredded, to garnish

crusty bread, to serve

Method

❶ Preheat the grill to hot. Halve and deseed the peppers, then arrange them on the grill rack and cook, turning occasionally, for 8–10 minutes, or until softened and charred.

❷ Leave to cool slightly, then peel off the charred skin. Reserving a small piece for the garnish, chop the pepper flesh and place in a large saucepan.

❸ Mix in the onion, celery and garlic. Add the stock and bay leaves. Bring to the boil, cover and simmer for 15 minutes. Remove the saucepan from the heat.

❹ Stir in the tomatoes and transfer to a food processor or blender. Process until smooth, then return to the saucepan.

❺ Season to taste with salt and pepper and heat for 3–4 minutes, or until piping hot. Ladle into warmed bowls and garnish with the reserved pepper cut into strips and the shredded spring onion floating on the top. Serve with crusty bread.

Cook's tip

If you prefer a coarser, more robust soup, lightly mash the tomatoes with a wooden spoon and omit the blending process in Step 4.

Nutritional Information

Calories	52	Sugars	9g
Protein	3g	Fat	0.4g
Carbohydrate	10g	Saturates	0g

Lentil & Ham Soup

This is a good hearty soup, based on a stock made from a ham knuckle, with plenty of vegetables and red lentils to thicken it and add flavour.

serves 4

225 g/8 oz red lentils

1.5 litres/2¾ pints stock or water

2 onions, chopped

1 garlic clove, crushed

2 large carrots, chopped

1 lean ham knuckle or 175 g/6 oz lean bacon, chopped

4 large tomatoes, peeled and chopped

2 fresh or dried bay leaves

250 g/9 oz potatoes, chopped

salt and pepper

1 tbsp white wine vinegar

¼ tsp ground allspice

chopped spring onions or chopped fresh parsley, to garnish

Method

❶ Place the lentils and stock in a large saucepan and leave to soak for 1–2 hours.

❷ Add the onions, garlic, carrots, ham knuckle, tomatoes and bay leaves and season to taste. Bring the mixture to the boil, cover and and leave to simmer for 1 hour, or until the lentils are tender, stirring occasionally to prevent the lentils sticking to the bottom of the saucepan.

❸ Add the potatoes and continue to simmer for 20 minutes, or until the potatoes and ham knuckle are tender.

❹ Discard the bay leaves. Remove the knuckle and chop 125 g/4½ oz of the meat and reserve. If liked, press half the soup through a sieve or process in a food processor or blender until smooth. Return to the saucepan with the rest of the soup.

❺ Taste and adjust the seasoning if necessary, add the vinegar and allspice and the reserved chopped ham. Simmer gently for a further 5–10 minutes. Garnish with spring onions and serve.

Nutritional Information

Calories 219
Protein 17g
Carbohydrate 33g
Sugars 4g
Fat 3g
Saturates 1g

Beef & Vegetable Soup

This comforting broth is perfect for a cold day and is just as delicious made with lean lamb or pork fillet.

serves 4

55 g/2 oz pearl barley, soaked overnight

1.2 litres/2 pints beef stock

1 tsp dried mixed herbs

225 g/8 oz lean rump or sirloin steak, trimmed and cut into strips

1 large carrot, diced

1 leek, shredded

1 onion, chopped

2 celery sticks, sliced

salt and pepper

2 tbsp chopped fresh parsley, to garnish

crusty bread, to serve

Method

❶ Place the pearl barley in a large, heavy-based saucepan. Pour the stock over and add the mixed herbs, then bring to the boil. Reduce the heat, cover and simmer gently over a low heat for 10 minutes.

❷ Skim away any scum that has risen to the top of the stock with a flat spoon. Add the steak, carrot, leek, onion and celery to the saucepan. Return to the boil, cover and leave to simmer for 1 hour, or until the barley, meat and vegetables are just tender.

❸ Skim away any remaining scum that has risen to the top of the soup with a flat ladle. Blot the surface with kitchen paper to remove any fat. Season to taste with salt and pepper.

❹ Ladle the soup into warmed soup bowls and sprinkle with chopped parsley. Serve piping hot with crusty bread.

Cook's tip

A delicious vegetarian version can be made by omitting the steak and beef stock and using vegetable stock instead. Just before serving, stir in 175 g/6 oz firm tofu, drained and diced.

Nutritional Information

Calories	138	Sugars	2g
Protein	13g	Fat	3g
Carbohydrate	15g	Saturates	1g

Yogurt & Spinach Soup

**Whole young spinach leaves add vibrant colour to this unusual soup.
Serve with hot, crusty bread for a nutritious light meal.**

serves 4

600 ml/1 pint chicken stock

salt and pepper

4 tbsp long-grain rice, rinsed and drained

4 tbsp water

1 tbsp cornflour

600 ml/1 pint low-fat natural yogurt

3 egg yolks, lightly beaten

juice of 1 lemon

350 g/12 oz young spinach leaves,
washed and drained

fresh crusty bread, to serve

Method

❶ Pour the stock into a large saucepan, season to taste with salt and pepper and bring to the boil. Add the rice and simmer for 10 minutes, or until barely cooked. Remove the saucepan from the heat.

❷ Mix the water and cornflour together until smooth. Pour the yogurt into a second saucepan and stir in the cornflour mixture. Set the saucepan over a low heat and bring to the boil, stirring with a wooden spoon in one direction only. This will stabilize the yogurt and prevent it separating or curdling on contact with the hot stock. When the yogurt has reached boiling point, stand the saucepan on a heat diffuser and simmer gently for

10 minutes. Remove the saucepan from the heat and leave to cool slightly before stirring in the beaten egg yolks.

❸ Pour the yogurt mixture into the stock, stir in the lemon juice and stir to blend thoroughly. Keep the soup warm, but do not let it boil.

❹ Blanch the spinach leaves in a large saucepan of salted boiling water for 2-3 minutes, or until they begin to soften but have not wilted. Tip the spinach into a colander, drain well and stir it into the soup. Warm through, then taste and adjust the seasoning if necessary. Serve in warmed soup bowls with crusty bread.

Nutritional Information

Calories	227	Sugars	13g
Protein	14g	Fat	7g
Carbohydrate	29g	Saturates	2g

Minted Onion Bhajis

Gram flour (also known as besan flour) is a fine yellow flour made from chickpeas and is available from supermarkets and Asian food shops.

makes 12

125 g/4½ oz gram flour

¼ tsp cayenne pepper

¼–½ tsp ground coriander

¼–½ tsp ground cumin

1 tbsp chopped fresh mint

4 tbsp Greek style yogurt

75 ml/2½ fl oz cold water

1 large onion, quartered and thinly sliced

vegetable oil, for frying

salt and pepper

fresh mint sprigs, to garnish

Method

❶ Place the gram flour in a bowl, add the cayenne, coriander, cumin and mint and season to taste with salt and pepper. Stir in the yogurt, water and sliced onion and mix well.

❷ Fill a large, deep frying pan one-third full of oil and heat until very hot. Carefully drop heaped spoonfuls of the mixture, a few at a time, into the hot oil and use 2 forks to neaten the mixture into rough ball shapes.

❸ Fry the bhajis until golden brown and cooked through, turning frequently.

❹ Drain the bhajis thoroughly on kitchen paper and keep them warm while cooking the remainder in the same way.

❺ Arrange the bhajis on a large serving plate and garnish with fresh mint sprigs. Serve hot or warm.

Cook's tip

Gram flour is excellent for making batter and is used in India in place of flour. It can be made from ground split peas as well as chickpeas.

Nutritional Information

Calories	251	Sugars	7g
Protein	7g	Fat	8g
Carbohydrate	39g	Saturates	1g

Chicken &
Almond Rissoles

Cooked potatoes and chicken are combined to make tasty nutty rissoles, which are served with stir-fried vegetables.

serves 4

115 g/4 oz parboiled potatoes, grated

1 carrot, grated

115 g/4 oz cooked chicken, minced

1 garlic clove, crushed

½ tsp dried tarragon or thyme

pinch of ground allspice or

ground coriander

salt and pepper

1 egg yolk or ½ egg, beaten

25 g/1 oz flaked almonds, finely chopped

butter, for greasing

lime wedges, to garnish

Stir-fried vegetables

1 tbsp groundnut oil

1 celery stick, thinly sliced diagonally

2 spring onions, thinly sliced diagonally

8 baby corn cobs

40 g/1½ oz mangetout or sugar snap peas

2 tsp balsamic vinegar

Method

❶ Preheat the oven to 200°C/400°F/ Gas Mark 6. Mix the potatoes, carrot and chicken with the garlic, herbs and spices and season. Add the egg and bind the ingredients together. Divide the mixture in half and shape into 'sausages'. Spread the almonds on a plate and coat each rissole in the nuts. Place the rissoles in a greased ovenproof dish and cook in the preheated oven for 20 minutes, or until browned.

❷ To stir-fry the vegetables, heat the oil in a frying pan. Add the celery and spring onions and cook over a high heat for 1–2 minutes, then add the corn cobs and mangetout and cook for a further 2–3 minutes. Add the vinegar.

❸ Transfer the rissoles and stir-fried vegetables to individual serving plates and garnish with lime wedges. Serve.

Nutritional Information

Calories	161	Sugars	3g
Protein	12g	Fat	9g
Carbohydrate	8g	Saturates	1g

Sweet & Sour Drumsticks

Chicken drumsticks are marinated to impart a tangy, sweet and sour flavour and a shiny glaze.

serves 4

8 chicken drumsticks

4 tbsp red wine vinegar

2 tbsp tomato purée

2 tbsp soy sauce

2 tbsp clear honey

1 tbsp Worcestershire sauce

1 garlic clove, crushed

good pinch of cayenne pepper

fresh parsley sprigs, to garnish

crisp salad, to serve

Method

❶ Skin the chicken drumsticks, if desired, and slash 2–3 times with a sharp knife. Arrange the drumsticks in a single layer in a shallow, non-metallic container.

❷ Mix the vinegar, tomato purée, soy sauce, honey, Worcestershire sauce, garlic and cayenne together in a small bowl and pour over the chicken drumsticks. Cover and leave to marinate in the refrigerator for 1 hour.

❸ Preheat the barbecue to medium. Cook the drumsticks over the hot coals for 20 minutes, brushing with the marinade and turning during cooking, until the chicken is tender and the juices run clear when a skewer is inserted into the thickest part of the meat. Garnish with parsley sprigs and serve with a crisp salad.

Cook's tip

For an extra tangy flavour, add the juice of 1 lime to the marinade. While the drumsticks are cooking, check regularly to ensure that they are not burning.

Nutritional Information

Calories 171	Sugars 9g
Protein 23g	Fat 5g
Carbohydrate 10g	Saturates 1g

Bruschetta

Traditionally, this Italian savoury is enriched with olive oil. Here, sun-dried tomatoes are a good substitute and only a little oil is used.

serves 4

55 g/2 oz dry-pack sun-dried tomatoes

300 ml/10 fl oz boiling water

35-cm/14-inch long Granary or wholemeal French baguette

1 large garlic clove, halved

25 g/1 oz black olives in brine, stoned, drained and quartered

2 tsp olive oil

salt and pepper

2 tbsp chopped fresh basil

40 g/1½ oz low-fat mozzarella cheese, grated

fresh basil leaves, to garnish

Method

1 Place the sun-dried tomatoes in a heatproof bowl and pour over the boiling water.

2 Leave to stand for 30 minutes to allow the tomatoes to soften. Drain well and pat dry with kitchen paper. Slice into thin strips and reserve.

3 Preheat the grill. Trim and discard the ends from the bread and cut into 12 slices. Arrange on a grill rack and cook under the hot grill for 1–2 minutes on each side, or until lightly golden.

4 Rub both sides of each piece of bread with the cut sides of the garlic. Top with the strips of sun-dried tomato and olives. Brush lightly with oil and season well with salt and pepper. Sprinkle with the basil and mozzarella cheese and return to the grill for 1–2 minutes, or until the cheese is bubbling and melted.

5 Transfer to a warmed serving plate and garnish with fresh basil leaves. Serve.

Nutritional Information

Calories	178	Sugars	2g
Protein	8g	Fat	6g
Carbohydrate	24g	Saturates	2g

Cheese & Chive Scones

These teatime classics have been given a healthy twist by the use of
low-fat soft cheese and reduced-fat Cheddar cheese.

makes 10

225 g/8 oz self-raising flour, plus extra
for dusting

1 tsp powdered mustard

½ tsp cayenne pepper

½ tsp salt

100 g/3½ oz low-fat soft cheese with
added herbs

2 tbsp snipped fresh chives, plus extra
to garnish

100 ml/3½ fl oz skimmed milk, plus extra
for brushing

55 g/2 oz reduced-fat mature
Cheddar cheese, grated

low-fat soft cheese, to serve

Method

❶ Preheat the oven to 200°C/400°F/ Gas Mark 6. Sift the flour, mustard, cayenne and salt into a large bowl. Add the soft cheese and mix together until well incorporated. Stir in the chives.

❷ Make a well in the centre of the ingredients and gradually stir in the milk until the mixture forms a soft dough.

❸ Turn the dough out on to a floured work surface and knead lightly. Roll out until 2 cm/¾ inch thick and use a 5-cm/ 2-inch plain pastry cutter to stamp out as many rounds as you can. Transfer the rounds to a baking sheet.

❹ Re-knead the dough trimmings together and roll out again. Stamp out more rounds – you should be able to make 10 scones in total.

❺ Brush the scones with milk and sprinkle with the grated cheese. Bake in the preheated oven for 15–20 minutes, or until risen and golden. Transfer the scones to a wire rack to cool.

❻ Serve the scones warm with low-fat soft cheese, garnished with chives.

Nutritional Information

Calories	297	Sugars	7g
Protein	13g	Fat	3g
Carbohydrate	49g	Saturates	4g

Potatoes with a Spicy Filling

The filling has the Middle Eastern flavours of chickpeas, cumin and coriander.

serves 4

4 large baking potatoes

1 tbsp vegetable oil (optional)

salt and pepper

430 g/15½ oz canned chickpeas, drained

1 tsp ground coriander

1 tsp ground cumin

4 tbsp chopped fresh coriander

150 ml/5 fl oz low-fat natural yogurt

Salad

2 tomatoes, chopped

½ cucumber, sliced

½ red onion, thinly sliced

Method

❶ Preheat the oven to 200°C/400°F/ Gas Mark 6. Scrub the potatoes and pat them dry with kitchen paper. Prick them all over with a fork, brush with oil, if using, and season. Place them on a large baking tray and bake in the oven for 1–1¼ hours, or until cooked through. Leave to cool for 10 minutes.

❷ Place the chickpeas in a large bowl and mash. Stir in the ground coriander, cumin and half the chopped coriander, then cover and reserve.

❸ Halve the potatoes and scoop the flesh into a bowl, keeping the shells intact. Mash the flesh until smooth and gently mix into the chickpea mixture with the yogurt. Season to taste. Place the shells on a baking tray and fill with the potato mixture. Return the potatoes to the oven and bake for 10–15 minutes, or until thoroughly heated through.

❹ Toss all the salad ingredients together. Sprinkle the potatoes with the remaining coriander and serve with the salad.

Nutritional Information

Calories	335	Sugars	7g
Protein	15g	Fat	7g
Carbohydrate	57g	Saturates	1g

Rice & Tuna Peppers

Grilled mixed sweet peppers are filled with tender tuna, sweetcorn, nutty brown and wild rice and grated reduced-fat Cheddar cheese.

serves 4

55 g/2 oz wild rice

55 g/2 oz brown rice

4 assorted peppers, halved and deseeded

200 g/7 oz canned tuna in brine, drained and flaked

325 g/11½ oz canned sweetcorn kernels, drained

100 g/3½ oz reduced-fat mature Cheddar cheese, grated

1 bunch fresh basil leaves, shredded

salt and pepper

2 tbsp dry white breadcrumbs

1 tbsp freshly grated Parmesan cheese

fresh basil leaves, to garnish

crisp salad leaves, to serve

Method

❶ Place the wild rice and brown rice in separate saucepans, pour over enough boiling water to cover and bring to the boil. Cook for 40–50 minutes, or according to the packet instructions, until tender. Drain the rice well.

❷ Meanwhile, preheat the grill to medium. Arrange the peppers on the grill rack, cut side down. Grill for 5 minutes, turn the peppers over and cook for a further 4–5 minutes.

❸ Place the cooked wild and brown rice in a large bowl and mix together. Add the flaked tuna and drained sweetcorn and gently fold in the grated cheese. Stir the basil leaves into the rice mixture and season to taste with salt and pepper.

❹ Divide the tuna and rice mixture into 8 equal portions. Pile one portion into each cooked pepper half. Mix the breadcrumbs and Parmesan cheese together and sprinkle over each pepper.

❺ Return the peppers to the grill for 4–5 minutes, or until hot and golden brown. Serve immediately, garnished with basil and accompanied with salad leaves.

Nutritional Information

Calories	332	Sugars	13g
Protein	27g	Fat	8g
Carbohydrate	42g	Saturates	4g

Red Mullet & Coconut Loaf

This fish and coconut loaf is ideal to take along on picnics because it can be served cold as well as hot.

serves 4-6

600 ml/1 pint coconut liquid (see Step 1)

225 g/8 oz red mullet fillets, skinned

2 tomatoes, deseeded and finely chopped

2 green peppers, finely chopped

1 onion, finely chopped

1 fresh red chilli, finely chopped

150 g/5½ oz breadcrumbs

salt and pepper

butter, for greasing

Hot pepper sauce

125 ml/4 fl oz tomato ketchup

1 tsp West Indian hot pepper sauce

¼ tsp hot mustard

To garnish

lemon twists

fresh chervil sprigs

Method

❶ Preheat the oven to 200°C/400°F/ Gas Mark 6. Using a hammer and the tip of a sturdy knife, poke out the 'eyes' in the top of a fresh coconut and pour the liquid into a jug. Finely chop the fish and mix with the tomatoes, peppers, onion and chilli. Stir in the breadcrumbs, coconut liquid and salt and pepper.

❷ Grease a 500-g/1 lb 2-oz loaf tin and line the base. Add the fish mixture.

❸ Bake the loaf in the preheated oven for 1–1¼ hours, or until set.

❹ To make the hot pepper sauce, mix the tomato ketchup, hot pepper sauce and mustard together in a bowl until smooth and creamy.

❺ Cut the loaf into slices, garnish with lemon twists and chervil and serve hot or cold with the sauce.

Nutritional Information

Calories	138	Sugars	12g
Protein	11g	Fat	1g
Carbohydrate	23g	Saturates	0g

Main Courses
& Side Dishes

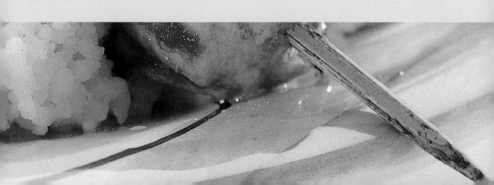

Thai Red Chicken

This is a really colourful dish, the red of the tomatoes perfectly complementing
the orange of the sweet potato.

serves 4

1 tbsp sunflower oil

450 g/1 lb lean boneless, skinless chicken

2 garlic cloves, crushed

2 tbsp Thai red curry paste

2 tbsp fresh grated galangal or

root ginger

1 tbsp tamarind paste

4 lime leaves

225 g/8 oz sweet potato

600 ml/1 pint coconut milk

225 g/8 oz cherry tomatoes, halved

3 tbsp chopped fresh coriander

freshly cooked jasmine or Thai fragrant

rice, to serve

Method

❶ Heat the oil in a preheated wok or
large, heavy-based saucepan.

❷ Thinly slice the chicken. Add the
chicken to the wok and stir-fry for
5 minutes.

❸ Add the garlic, curry paste, galangal,
tamarind paste and lime leaves to the wok
and stir-fry for 1 minute.

❹ Using a sharp knife, peel and dice the
sweet potato. Add the coconut milk and
sweet potato to the mixture in the wok
and bring to the boil. Leave to bubble over
a medium heat for 20 minutes, or until
the juices begin to thicken and reduce.

❺ Add the cherry tomatoes and chopped
coriander to the curry and cook for a
further 5 minutes, stirring occasionally.
Transfer to serving plates and serve hot
with freshly cooked rice.

Nutritional Information

Calories	249	Sugars	14g
Protein	26g	Fat	7g
Carbohydrate	22g	Saturates	2g

Jerk Chicken

This is perhaps one of the best known Caribbean dishes. The 'jerk' in the name refers to the hot spicy coating.

serves 4

4 lean chicken portions

1 bunch spring onions

1–2 fresh Scotch Bonnet chillies, deseeded

1 garlic clove

5-cm/2-inch piece fresh root ginger, roughly chopped

½ tsp dried thyme

½ tsp paprika

¼ tsp ground allspice

pinch of ground cinnamon

pinch of ground cloves

4 tbsp white wine vinegar

3 tbsp light soy sauce

pepper

Method

❶ Place the chicken portions in a shallow, non-metallic dish.

❷ Place the spring onions, chillies, garlic, ginger, thyme, paprika, allspice, cinnamon, cloves, wine vinegar, soy sauce and pepper to taste in a food processor and process until smooth.

❸ Pour the spicy mixture over the chicken. Turn the chicken portions over so that they are well coated in the marinade.

❹ Transfer the chicken portions to the refrigerator and leave to marinate for up to 24 hours.

❺ Preheat the barbecue. Remove the chicken from the marinade and barbecue over medium–hot coals for 30 minutes, turning the chicken over and basting occasionally with the marinade, until the chicken is browned and cooked through.

❻ Transfer the chicken portions to individual serving plates and serve.

Nutritional Information

Calories	158	Sugars	0.4g
Protein	29g	Fat	4g
Carbohydrate	2g	Saturates	1g

Ginger Chicken & Corn

Chicken wings and corn in a sticky ginger marinade are designed to be eaten with the fingers – there's no other way!

serves 4

3 fresh corn cobs

12 chicken wings

2.5-cm/1-inch piece fresh root ginger

6 tbsp lemon juice

4 tsp sunflower oil

1 tbsp golden caster sugar

To serve

jacket potatoes

mixed salad leaves

Method

❶ Preheat the grill to medium. Remove the husks and silken hairs from the corn cobs. Using a sharp knife, cut each cob into 6 slices. Place in a large bowl with the chicken wings.

❷ Peel the piece of root ginger and grate or chop fincly.

❸ Mix the ginger, lemon juice, sunflower oil and sugar together in a bowl, then pour over the corn and chicken and toss until evenly coated.

❹ Thread the corn and chicken onto 6 metal skewers, to make turning easier.

❺ Cook the corn and chicken skewers under the hot grill, basting with the gingery glaze and turning frequently for 15–20 minutes, or until the corn is golden brown and tender and the chicken is cooked through. Alternatively, cook on a barbecue over hot coals. Serve with jacket potatoes and a salad.

Nutritional Information

Calories	123	Sugars	3g
Protein	14g	Fat	6g
Carbohydrate	3g	Saturates	1g

Skewered Spicy Tomato Chicken

These low-fat, spicy skewers are cooked in a matter of minutes. They can be assembled ahead of time and stored in the refrigerator until you need them.

serves 4

500 g/1 lb 2 oz skinless, boneless chicken breasts

3 tbsp tomato purée

2 tbsp Worcestershire sauce

2 tbsp clear honey

1 tbsp chopped fresh rosemary

250 g/9 oz cherry tomatoes

fresh rosemary sprigs, to garnish

freshly cooked couscous or rice, to serve

Method

❶ Preheat the grill to medium. Using a sharp knife, cut the chicken into 2.5-cm/1-inch chunks and place in a bowl.

❷ Mix the tomato purée, Worcestershire sauce, honey and chopped rosemary together in a separate bowl. Add to the chicken, stirring to coat evenly.

❸ Thread the chicken pieces and cherry tomatoes alternately onto 8 presoaked wooden skewers, then spoon over any remaining glaze.

❹ Cook the skewers under the hot grill for 8–10 minutes, turning occasionally, until the chicken is cooked through. Serve immediately on a bed of couscous, garnished with rosemary sprigs.

Nutritional Information

Calories	195	Sugars	11g
Protein	28g	Fat	4g
Carbohydrate	12g	Saturates	1g

Teppanyaki

This simple, Japanese style of cooking is ideal for thinly sliced breast of chicken.
Mirin is a rich, sweet rice wine, which is available from Asian food shops.

serves 4

4 boneless chicken breasts	100 g/3½ oz beansprouts
1 red pepper	1 tbsp sunflower oil
1 green pepper	4 tbsp soy sauce
4 spring onions	4 tbsp mirin
8 baby corn cobs	1 tbsp grated fresh root ginger

Method

❶ Using a sharp knife, remove the skin from the chicken and slice at a slight angle, to a thickness of about 5 mm/ ¼ inch.

❷ Deseed and thinly slice the peppers and slice the spring onions and baby corn cobs. Arrange the peppers, spring onions, baby corn cobs and beansprouts on a plate with the sliced chicken.

❸ Heat a large grill pan or heavy-based frying pan, then lightly brush with oil. Add the vegetables and chicken slices in small batches, allowing space between them so that they cook thoroughly.

❹ Mix the soy sauce, mirin and ginger together in a small bowl and serve as a dip with the chicken and vegetables.

Variation

If you cannot find mirin, add 1 tablespoon of soft brown sugar to the sauce instead. Instead of serving the sauce as a dip, you could use it as a marinade. However, do not leave it to marinate for more than 2 hours, otherwise the soy sauce will cause the chicken to dry out and become tough. Use other vegetables, such as mangetout or thinly sliced carrots, if you prefer.

Nutritional Information

Calories	206	Sugars	4g
Protein	30g	Fat	7g
Carbohydrate	6g	Saturates	2g

Beef Teriyaki

This Japanese-style teriyaki sauce complements barbecued beef, but it can also be used to accompany chicken or salmon.

serves 4

450 g/1 lb extra thin lean beef steaks

8 spring onions, cut into short lengths

1 yellow pepper, deseeded and cut into chunks

green salad, to serve

Sauce

1 tsp cornflour

2 tbsp dry sherry

2 tbsp white wine vinegar

3 tbsp soy sauce

1 tbsp dark muscovado sugar

1 garlic clove, crushed

½ tsp ground cinnamon

½ tsp ground ginger

Method

❶ Place the beef in a shallow, non-metallic dish. To make the sauce, mix the cornflour with the sherry until smooth. Place the vinegar, soy sauce, sugar, garlic, cinnamon and ginger in a bowl and stir in the cornflour paste. Pour over the beef, turn to coat and chill for 2 hours.

❷ Preheat the barbecue. Remove the beef from the sauce, draining well. Pour the sauce into a saucepan.

❸ Cut the beef into thin strips and thread these, concertina-style, on to several presoaked wooden skewers, alternating each strip of beef with pieces of spring onion and yellow pepper.

❹ Gently heat the sauce until it is just simmering, stirring occasionally. Barbecue the kebabs over hot coals for 5–8 minutes, turning and basting the beef and vegetables occasionally with the reserved teriyaki sauce.

❺ Arrange the skewers on serving plates and pour the remaining sauce over the kebabs. Serve immediately with salad.

Nutritional Information

Calories	184	Sugars	6g
Protein	24g	Fat	5g
Carbohydrate	8g	Saturates	2g

Wine-marinated Steaks

Fillet, sirloin, rump and entrecôte are all suitable cuts of steak for this dish, although rump steak retains the most flavour.

serves 4

4 rump steaks, about 250 g/9 oz each	**Marinade**
4 large field mushrooms	600 ml/1 pint red wine
olive oil, for brushing	1 onion, cut into quarters
branch of fresh rosemary (optional)	2 tbsp Dijon mustard
	2 garlic cloves, crushed
	salt and pepper

Method

❶ Snip through the fat strip on the steaks in 3 places, so that the steak retains its shape when cooked.

❷ Mix the red wine, onion, mustard, garlic and salt and pepper together in a bowl. Lay the steaks in a shallow, non-metallic dish and pour over the marinade. Cover and leave to chill for 2–3 hours. Remove the steaks from the refrigerator 30 minutes before cooking, to let them come to room temperature.

❸ Preheat the barbecue. Cook the steaks over hot coals for 1 minute on each side. If the steaks are 2.5 cm/1 inch thick, keep them over the hot barbecue and cook for 4 minutes on each side for medium-rare steaks, or to taste. If the steaks are thicker, move them further away from the coals. To test the readiness of the steaks while cooking, press them with your finger – the more the steak yields, the less it is cooked.

❹ Brush the mushrooms with oil. Cook them alongside the steaks for 5 minutes, turning once. Meanwhile, place the rosemary, if using, in the fire to flavour the steaks.

❺ Remove the steaks from the barbecue and leave to rest for 1–2 minutes. Slice the mushrooms and serve immediately with the steaks.

Nutritional Information

Calories	356	Sugars	2g
Protein	41g	Fat	9g
Carbohydrate	2g	Saturates	4g

Pork Stroganoff

Tender, lean pork is cooked in a tasty, rich tomato sauce and flavoured with a tangy natural yogurt.

serves 4

1 tbsp vegetable oil

350 g/12 oz lean pork fillet, cut into 1-cm/½-inch thick slices

1 onion, chopped

2 garlic cloves, crushed

25 g/1 oz plain flour

2 tbsp tomato purée

425 ml/15 fl oz chicken or vegetable stock

125 g/4½ oz button mushrooms, sliced

1 large green pepper, halved, deseeded and diced

½ tsp ground nutmeg

salt and pepper

4 tbsp low-fat natural yogurt, plus extra to serve

freshly cooked rice, to serve

To garnish

chopped fresh parsley

ground nutmeg

Method

❶ Heat the oil in a large, heavy-based saucepan. Add the pork, onion and garlic and gently fry for 4–5 minutes, or until they are lightly browned.

❷ Add the flour and tomato purée, then pour in the stock and stir until mixed thoroughly.

❸ Add the mushrooms, green pepper and nutmeg. Season to taste and bring to the boil. Reduce the heat, cover and leave to simmer for 20 minutes, or until the pork is tender and cooked through.

❹ Remove the saucepan from the heat and stir in the yogurt.

❺ Serve the pork and sauce on a bed of rice, sprinkled with chopped parsley, with an extra spoonful of yogurt and a light dusting of ground nutmeg.

Nutritional Information

Calories 223

Protein 22g

Carbohydrate 12g

Sugars 7g

Fat 10g

Saturates 3g

Tangy Pork Fillet

These tasty pork fillets are served with a delicious tangy orange sauce.

serves 4

400 g/14 oz lean pork fillet

salt and pepper

3 tbsp orange marmalade

grated rind and juice of 1 orange

1 tbsp white wine vinegar

dash of Tabasco sauce

To serve

freshly cooked rice

mixed salad leaves

Sauce

1 tbsp olive oil

1 small onion, chopped

1 small green pepper, halved, deseeded
and thinly sliced

1 tbsp cornflour

150 ml/5 fl oz orange juice

Method

❶ Preheat the barbecue. Place a large piece of double-thickness foil in a shallow dish. Place the pork in the centre of the foil and season with salt and pepper.

❷ Heat the marmalade, orange rind and juice, vinegar and Tabasco together, stirring until the marmalade melts. Pour over the pork and wrap securely in the foil. Cook over hot coals for 25 minutes, turning occasionally.

❸ To make the sauce, heat the oil in a heavy-based saucepan. Add the onion and cook for 2–3 minutes. Add the green pepper and cook for 3–4 minutes.

❹ Remove the pork from the foil and place on the rack. Pour the juices from the pork into the saucepan with the sauce. Barbecue the pork for 10–20 minutes, turning, until cooked through.

❺ Mix the cornflour and orange juice together until smooth. Add to the sauce and cook, stirring, until the sauce has thickened. Slice the pork, spoon the sauce over and serve with rice and salad leaves.

Nutritional Information

Calories	230	Sugars	16g
Protein	19g	Fat	9g
Carbohydrate	20g	Saturates	3g

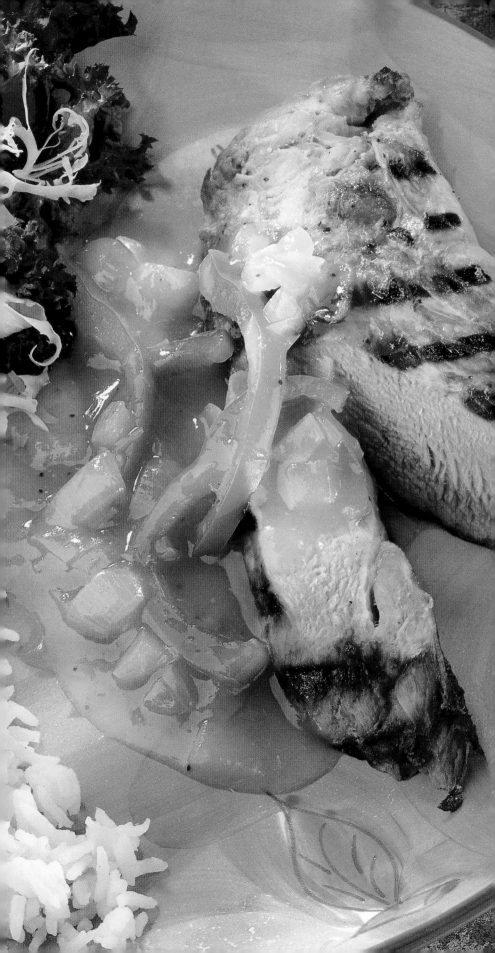

Savoury Hotpot

This hearty lamb stew is full of vegetables and herbs, and is topped
with a layer of crisp, golden potato slices – a satisfying family meal.

serves 4

8 middle neck lean lamb chops, neck
of lamb or any lean stewing lamb

salt and pepper

1–2 garlic cloves, crushed

2 lamb's kidneys (optional)

1 large onion, thinly sliced

1 leek, sliced

2–3 carrots, sliced

1 tsp chopped fresh tarragon or sage,
or ½ tsp dried tarragon or sage

1 kg/2 lb 4 oz potatoes, thinly sliced

300 ml/10 fl oz stock

2 tbsp margarine, melted, plus extra for
greasing, or 1 tbsp vegetable oil

chopped fresh parsley, to garnish

Method

❶ Preheat the oven to 180°C/350°F/
Gas Mark 4. Trim any excess fat from
the lamb and season well with salt and
pepper. Arrange in a large, ovenproof
casserole and sprinkle with the garlic.

❷ If using kidneys, remove the skin, halve
and cut out the cores. Chop into small
pieces and sprinkle them over the lamb.

❸ Place the vegetables over the lamb,
allowing the pieces to slip in between the
meat, then sprinkle with the herbs.
Arrange the potato on top of the meat
and vegetables, in an overlapping pattern.

❹ Bring the stock to the boil, season to
taste with salt and pepper, then pour over
the casserole. Brush the potatoes with the
melted margarine, cover with greased foil
or a lid and cook in the preheated oven
for 1½ hours.

❺ Remove the foil from the casserole,
increase the temperature to 220°C/425°F/
Gas Mark 7 and return the casserole to
the oven for 30 minutes, or until the
potatoes are browned.

❻ Garnish the hotpot with chopped
parsley and serve immediately.

Nutritional Information

Calories	365	Sugars	5g
Protein	23g	Fat	11g
Carbohydrate	48g	Saturates	4g

Baked Sea Bass

Sea bass is often paired with subtle Asian flavours. Serve the fish with pickled
sushi ginger and soy sauce, if liked.

serves 4

sunflower oil, for brushing (optional)

2 sea bass, about 1 kg/2 lb 4 oz each,
gutted and scaled

2 spring onions, green part only,
cut into strips

5-cm/2-inch piece fresh root ginger,
cut into strips

2 garlic cloves, unpeeled, lightly crushed

2 tbsp mirin or dry sherry

salt and pepper

To serve

pickled sushi ginger (optional)

soy sauce

Method

❶ Preheat the barbecue. Lay out a double thickness of foil and oil the top piece or lay a piece of baking paper over the foil.

❷ Place the fish in the middle of the foil and open the cavities. Push a mixture of spring onion, ginger and garlic between each cavity.

❸ Pour the mirin over the fish and season to taste with salt and pepper.

❹ Close the cavities and lay each fish on its side. Fold over the foil to encase the fish and seal the edges securely. Fold each end neatly.

❺ Cook over medium–hot coals for 15 minutes, turning once.

❻ To serve, remove the foil and cut each fish into 2–3 pieces. Serve with the pickled sushi ginger, if using, and soy sauce.

Nutritional Information

Calories	140	Sugars	0.1g
Protein	29g	Fat	1g
Carbohydrate	0.1g	Saturates	0.2g

Lemony Monkfish Skewers

A simple basting sauce is brushed over these tasty kebabs. When served with crusty bread and a green salad, they make a perfect light meal.

serves 4

450 g/1 lb monkfish tail, cut into
5-cm/2-inch chunks
2 courgettes, thickly sliced
1 lemon, cut into wedges
12 cherry tomatoes
8 bay leaves

Sauce
3 tbsp olive oil
2 tbsp lemon juice
1 tsp chopped fresh thyme
½ tsp lemon pepper
salt

To serve
green salad leaves
fresh crusty bread

Method

❶ Preheat the barbecue. Thread the monkfish, courgettes, lemon, tomatoes and bay leaves alternately onto 4 metal skewers.

❷ To make the basting sauce, mix the oil, lemon juice, thyme, lemon pepper and salt to taste together in a small bowl. Brush the sauce liberally over the kebabs.

❸ Cook the kebabs over medium–hot coals for 15 minutes, basting them frequently with the sauce, until the fish is cooked through. Transfer the skewers to individual serving plates and serve with green salad leaves and crusty bread.

Nutritional Information

Calories	191	Sugars	2g
Protein	21g	Fat	11g
Carbohydrate	1g	Saturates	1g

Charred Tuna Steaks

Tuna has a firm flesh, which is ideal for barbecuing, but it can be a little dry unless marinated first.

serves 4

4 tuna steaks

3 tbsp light soy sauce

1 tbsp Worcestershire sauce

1 tsp wholegrain mustard

1 tsp caster sugar

1 tbsp sunflower oil

green salad, to serve

To garnish

fresh flat-leaved parsley sprigs

lemon wedges

Method

❶ Arrange the tuna steaks in a single layer in a shallow dish.

❷ Mix the soy sauce, Worcestershire sauce, mustard, sugar and oil together in a small bowl. Pour the marinade over the tuna steaks and gently turn the tuna steaks to coat well.

❸ Cover and leave to marinate in the refrigerator for at least 30 minutes, or up to 2 hours.

❹ Preheat the barbecue. Remove the tuna steaks from the marinade, reserving it for basting. Cook over hot coals for

10–15 minutes, turning once and basting frequently with the reserved marinade.

❺ Transfer the tuna steaks to warmed serving plates. Garnish with flat-leaved parsley and lemon wedges and serve immediately with a green salad.

Cook's tip

If a marinade contains soy sauce, the marinating time should be limited, usually to 2 hours, to prevent the fish from drying out and becoming tough.

Nutritional Information

Calories	153	Sugars	1g
Protein	29g	Fat	3g
Carbohydrate	1g	Saturates	1g

Seafood Stir-fry

This combination of assorted seafood and tender vegetables flavoured
with ginger makes an ideal light meal served with egg noodles.

serves 4

100 g/3½ oz small, thin asparagus spears

1 tbsp sunflower oil

2.5-cm/1-inch piece fresh root ginger,
cut into thin strips

1 leek, shredded

2 carrots, cut into very thin strips

100 g/3½ oz baby corn cobs, cut into
quarters lengthways

2 tbsp light soy sauce

1 tbsp oyster sauce

1 tsp clear honey

450 g/1 lb cooked assorted shellfish,
thawed if frozen

freshly cooked egg noodles, to serve

To garnish

4 cooked large prawns

small bunch snipped fresh chives

Method

❶ Bring a small saucepan of water to
the boil. Add the asparagus and blanch
for 1–2 minutes. Drain the asparagus
and keep warm.

❷ Heat the oil in a preheated wok or large
frying pan. Add the ginger, leek, carrots
and corn cobs and cook for 3 minutes. Do
not let the vegetables brown.

❸ Add the soy sauce, oyster sauce and
honey to the wok.

❹ Add the cooked shellfish and continue
to cook, stirring, for 2–3 minutes, or until
the vegetables are just tender and the
shellfish are thoroughly heated through.
Add the blanched asparagus and cook for
2 minutes.

❺ To serve, pile the cooked noodles onto
4 warmed serving plates and spoon the
seafood stir-fry over them. Garnish with
the cooked large prawns and snipped
chives and serve immediately.

Nutritional Information

Calories	226	Sugars	5g
Protein	35g	Fat	7g
Carbohydrate	6g	Saturates	1g

Biryani with Onions

An assortment of vegetables is cooked here with tender rice, flavoured and coloured with bright yellow turmeric and other warming Indian spices.

serves 4

175 g/6 oz basmati rice, rinsed

55 g/2 oz red lentils, rinsed

1 bay leaf

6 cardamom pods, split

1 tsp ground turmeric

6 whole cloves

1 tsp cumin seeds

1 cinnamon stick, broken

1 onion, chopped

225 g/8 oz cauliflower florets

1 large carrot, diced

100 g/3½ oz frozen peas

55 g/2 oz sultanas

salt and pepper

600 ml/1 pint vegetable stock

naan bread, to serve

Caramelized onions

2 tsp vegetable oil

1 red onion, shredded

1 onion, shredded

2 tsp caster sugar

Method

❶ Place the rice, lentils, bay leaf, spices, onion, cauliflower, carrot, peas and sultanas in a large saucepan. Season to taste with salt and pepper and mix well.

❷ Pour in the stock and bring to the boil. Reduce the heat, cover and simmer for 15 minutes, stirring occasionally, or until the rice is tender. Remove the saucepan from the heat and leave, covered, for 10 minutes. Discard the bay leaf, cardamoms, cloves and cinnamon stick.

❸ To make the caramelized onions, heat the oil in a frying pan. Add the onions and fry them over a medium heat for 3–4 minutes, or until softened. Add the sugar, increase the heat and cook, stirring constantly, for a further 2–3 minutes, until the onions are golden.

❹ Gently mix the rice and vegetables together and transfer to warmed serving plates. Spoon over the onions and serve immediately with naan bread.

Nutritional Information

Calories	223	Sugars	18g
Protein	8g	Fat	4g
Carbohydrate	42g	Saturates	1g

Moroccan Salad

Couscous is a type of semolina made from durum wheat. It is wonderful in salads, as it readily absorbs the flavour of the dressing.

serves 4

175 g/6 oz couscous

1 bunch spring onions, finely chopped

1 small green pepper, halved, deseeded and chopped

10-cm/4-inch piece cucumber, chopped

175 g/6 oz canned chickpeas, drained and rinsed

55 g/2 oz sultanas or raisins

salt and pepper

few lettuce leaves

2 oranges, peeled and segmented

fresh mint sprigs, to garnish

Dressing

rind of 1 orange, finely grated

1 tbsp chopped fresh mint

150 ml/5 fl oz natural yogurt

Method

❶ Place the couscous in a bowl and pour over enough boiling water to cover. Leave to soak for 15 minutes, until the grains are tender, then stir gently with a fork to separate them.

❷ Add the spring onions, green pepper, cucumber, chickpeas and sultanas to the couscous, stirring well. Season to taste with salt and pepper.

❸ To make the dressing, place the orange rind, mint and yogurt in a small bowl and mix together until well blended. Pour the

dressing over the couscous mixture and stir to mix well.

❹ Arrange the lettuce leaves on 4 serving plates. Divide the couscous mixture between the plates and arrange the orange segments on top. Garnish with fresh mint sprigs and serve.

Nutritional Information

Calories	195	Sugars	15g
Protein	8g	Fat	2g
Carbohydrate	40g	Saturates	0.3g

Mushroom Cannelloni

Thick pasta tubes are filled with a mixture of seasoned chopped mushrooms and baked in a rich, fragrant tomato sauce.

serves 4

350 g/12 oz chestnut mushrooms, finely chopped

1 onion, finely chopped

1 garlic clove, crushed

1 tbsp chopped fresh thyme

½ tsp freshly grated nutmeg

4 tbsp dry white wine

50 g/1¾ oz fresh white breadcrumbs

salt and pepper

12 dried 'quick-cook' cannelloni tubes

shavings of fresh Parmesan cheese, to garnish (optional)

Tomato sauce

1 large red pepper, halved and deseeded

200 ml/7 fl oz dry white wine

450 ml/16 fl oz passata

2 tbsp tomato purée

2 bay leaves

1 tsp caster sugar

Method

❶ Preheat the oven to 200°C/400°F/ Gas Mark 6 and preheat the grill. Place the mushrooms, onion and garlic in a saucepan. Stir in the thyme, nutmeg and wine. Bring to the boil, cover and simmer for 10 minutes. Stir in the breadcrumbs and season to taste. Cool for 10 minutes.

❷ To make the sauce, place the pepper on a grill rack and cook under the hot grill for 8–10 minutes, until charred. Cool, then peel off the skin. Chop the flesh and place in a food processor with the wine. Blend

until smooth, then pour into a saucepan. Add the remaining sauce ingredients and mix. Bring to the boil and simmer for 10 minutes. Discard the bay leaves.

❸ Cover the base of a large, ovenproof dish with a thin layer of sauce. Fill the cannelloni with the mushroom mixture and place in a single layer in the dish. Spoon over the remaining sauce, then cover and bake in the oven for 35–40 minutes. Garnish with Parmesan cheese shavings, if using, and serve.

Nutritional Information

Calories	156	Sugars	8g
Protein	6g	Fat	1g
Carbohydrate	21g	Saturates	0.2g

Desserts

Spun Sugar Pears

Whole pears are poached in a Madeira syrup in the microwave, then served with a delicate spun sugar surround.

serves 4

150 ml/5 fl oz water

150 ml/5 fl oz sweet Madeira wine

115 g/4 oz caster sugar

2 tbsp lime juice

4 ripe pears, peeled, stalks left on

fresh mint sprigs, to decorate

Spun sugar

115 g/4 oz caster sugar

3 tbsp water

Method

❶ Blend the water, Madeira, sugar and lime juice together in a large bowl. Cover and cook on High power for 3 minutes. Stir well until the sugar dissolves.

❷ Cut a thin slice from the base of each pear, so that they stand upright. Add the pears to the bowl, spooning the wine syrup over them. Cover and cook on High power for 10 minutes, until they are tender. Leave to cool, covered, in the syrup.

❸ Remove the pears from the syrup and leave to stand on serving plates. Cook the syrup, uncovered, on High power for 15 minutes, until reduced by half and

thickened slightly. Leave for 5 minutes, then spoon the syrup over the pears.

❹ To make the spun sugar, mix the sugar and water together in a bowl. Cook, uncovered, on High power for 1½ minutes. Stir until the sugar has dissolved completely. Continue to cook on High power for a further 5–6 minutes, until the sugar has caramelized.

❺ Wait for the caramel bubbles to subside and leave to stand for 2 minutes. Dip a teaspoon in the caramel and spin sugar around each pear in a circular motion. Decorate with mint sprigs and serve.

Nutritional Information

Calories	166	Sugars	41g
Protein	0.3g	Fat	0g
Carbohydrate	41g	Saturates	0g

Summer Fruit Clafoutis

Serve this mouthwatering French-style fruit-in-batter pudding hot or cold with
low-fat fromage frais or yogurt.

serves 4

500 g/1 lb 2 oz prepared fresh assorted
soft fruits, such as blackberries, raspberries,
strawberries, blueberries, gooseberries,
redcurrants and blackcurrants

4 tbsp soft fruit liqueur, such as kirsch,
crème de cassis or framboise

4 tbsp skimmed milk powder

115 g/4 oz plain flour

pinch of salt

55 g/2 oz caster sugar

2 eggs, beaten

300 ml/10 fl oz skimmed milk

1 tsp vanilla essence

2 tsp caster sugar, for dusting

To serve

assorted soft fruits

low-fat yogurt or natural fromage frais

Method

❶ Place the assorted soft fruits in a large
bowl and spoon over the fruit liqueur.
Cover and leave to chill for 1 hour for the
fruit to macerate.

❷ Mix the skimmed milk powder, flour,
salt and sugar together in a bowl. Make a
well in the centre and, using a balloon
whisk, gradually whisk in the eggs, milk
and vanilla essence until smooth. Transfer
to a jug and reserve for 30 minutes.

❸ Preheat the oven to 200°C/400°F/
Gas Mark 6. Line the base of a 23-cm/
9-inch round ovenproof dish with baking
paper, and spoon in the fruits and juices.

❹ Whisk the batter again and pour it
over the fruits, stand the dish on a baking
sheet and bake in the preheated oven
for 50 minutes, or until firm, risen and
golden brown.

❺ Dust with caster sugar. Serve
immediately with extra fruits and yogurt.

Nutritional Information

Calories 228
Protein 9g
Carbohydrate 42g

Sugars 26g
Fat 2g
Saturates 1g

Summer Fruit Salad

A mixture of soft summer fruits in an orange-flavoured syrup with a dash of port, served with low-fat fromage frais.

serves 6

85 g/3 oz caster sugar

5 tbsp water

grated rind and juice of 1 small orange

250 g/9 oz redcurrants, stripped from
their stalks

2 tsp arrowroot

2 tbsp port

115 g/4 oz blackberries

115 g/4 oz blueberries

115 g/4 oz strawberries

225 g/8 oz raspberries

low-fat fromage frais, to serve

Method

❶ Place the sugar, water and grated orange rind in a heavy-based saucepan and heat gently, stirring until the sugar has dissolved.

❷ Add the redcurrants and orange juice, bring to the boil and simmer gently for 2–3 minutes.

❸ Sieve the fruit, reserving the syrup, and place in a bowl.

❹ Blend the arrowroot with a little water. Return the syrup to the saucepan, add the arrowroot and bring to the boil, stirring constantly until thickened.

❺ Add the port and mix well. Pour the syrup over the redcurrants in the bowl.

❻ Add the blackberries, blueberries, strawberries and raspberries to the bowl. Mix the fruit together and leave to cool until required.

❼ Serve in individual glass dishes with fromage frais.

Nutritional Information

Calories	110	Sugars	26g
Protein	1g	Fat	0.1g
Carbohydrate	26g	Saturates	0g

Fruity Muffins

Perfect for those on a low-fat diet and for weight watchers, these little cakes contain no butter, just a little corn oil.

makes 10

225 g/8 oz wholemeal self-raising flour

2 tsp baking powder

25 g/1 oz light muscovado sugar

100 g/3½ oz ready-to-eat dried apricots, finely chopped

1 banana, mashed with 1 tbsp orange juice

1 tsp finely grated orange rind

300 ml/10 fl oz skimmed milk

1 egg, beaten

3 tbsp corn oil

2 tbsp porridge oats

fruit spread, honey or maple syrup, to serve

Method

❶ Preheat the oven to 200°C/400°F/ Gas Mark 6. Place 10 paper muffin cases in a deep patty tin. Sift the flour and baking powder into a large bowl, adding any bran that remains in the sieve. Stir in the sugar and apricots.

❷ Make a well in the centre of the dry ingredients and add the mashed banana, orange rind, milk, beaten egg and oil. Mix together to form a thick batter.

❸ Divide the batter evenly between the 10 paper cases. Sprinkle the tops with a few porridge oats and bake in the preheated oven for 25–30 minutes, or until well risen and firm to the touch or until a skewer inserted into the centre comes out clean. Transfer the muffins to a wire rack to cool slightly. Serve the muffins while they are warm with a little fruit spread.

Nutritional Information

Calories	162	Sugars	11g
Protein	4g	Fat	4g
Carbohydrate	28g	Saturates	1g

Strawberry Meringues

The combination of aromatic strawberries and rosewater with crisp caramelized sugar meringues makes this a truly irresistible dessert.

serves 4

3 egg whites

pinch of salt

175 g/6 oz light muscovado sugar, crushed

225 g/8 oz strawberries, hulled

2 tsp rosewater

150 ml/5 fl oz low-fat natural fromage frais

extra strawberries, to serve

(optional)

To decorate

rose petals

rose-scented geranium leaves

Method

❶ Preheat the oven to 120°C/250°F/ Gas Mark ½. Whisk the egg whites and salt together in a clean bowl until very stiff and dry. Gradually whisk in the sugar, a spoonful at a time, until stiff again.

❷ Line a baking sheet with baking paper and drop 12 spoonfuls of the meringue mixture on to it. Bake in the preheated oven for 3–3½ hours, until completely dried out and crisp. Leave to cool.

❸ Reserve 55 g/2 oz of the strawberries. Place the remaining strawberries in a food processor or blender and process for a few seconds until smooth.

❹ Alternatively, mash the strawberries with a fork and press through a sieve to form a purée. Stir in the rosewater. Leave to chill until required.

❺ To serve, slice the reserved strawberries lengthways. Sandwich the meringues together with fromage frais and sliced strawberries.

❻ Spoon the strawberry rose purée on to 6 serving plates and top with a meringue. Decorate with rose petals and rose-scented geranium leaves and serve with extra strawberries, if using.

Nutritional Information

Calories	145	Sugars	35g
Protein	3g	Fat	0.3g
Carbohydrate	35g	Saturates	0.1g

Almond Trifles

These trifles can be made with any type of fruit, even frozen. When they thaw, the juices will soak into the biscuit base – delicious!

serves 4

8 amaretti biscuits, crushed

4 tbsp brandy or Amaretto liqueur

225 g/8 oz raspberries

300 ml/10 fl oz canned low-fat custard

1 tsp almond essence

300 ml/10 fl oz low-fat natural fromage frais

15 g/½ oz toasted flaked almonds

1 tsp cocoa powder

Method

❶ Divide the amaretti biscuits between 4 dessert glasses. Sprinkle over the brandy and leave to stand for 30 minutes, until softened.

❷ Top the biscuits with a layer of raspberries, reserving a few for decoration, and spoon over enough custard just to cover.

❸ Mix the almond essence and fromage frais together and spoon the mixture over the custard, smoothing the surface. Leave to chill in the refrigerator for 30 minutes.

❹ Before serving, sprinkle with toasted almonds and dust with cocoa powder.

❺ Decorate the trifles with the reserved raspberries and serve immediately.

Nutritional Information

Calories	241	Sugars	23g
Protein	9g	Fat	6g
Carbohydrate	35g	Saturates	2g

Mixed Fruit Brûlées

Traditionally a rich mixture made with cream, this fruit-based version is just as tempting using low-fat soured cream and fromage frais as a topping.

serves 4

450 g/1 lb prepared assorted summer
fruits, such as strawberries, raspberries,
blackcurrants, redcurrants and cherries,
thawed if frozen
150 ml/5 fl oz soured cream

150 ml/5 fl oz low-fat natural
fromage frais
1 tsp vanilla essence
4 tbsp demerara sugar

Method

❶ Preheat the grill. Divide the prepared strawberries, raspberries, blackcurrants, redcurrants and cherries evenly between 4 small heatproof ramekin dishes.

❷ Mix the soured cream, fromage frais and vanilla essence together, then spoon over the fruit, to cover it completely.

❸ Top each serving with 1 tablespoon of demerara sugar and place the desserts under the hot grill for 2–3 minutes, until the sugar melts completely and begins to caramelize. Leave the mixed fruit brûlées to stand for 2 minutes before serving.

Cook's tip

Vegetarians should read the labels carefully when buying low-fat products, such as fromage frais, as some brands are thickened with non-vegetarian gelatine and other additives.

Nutritional Information

Calories	165	Sugars	21g
Protein	5g	Fat	7g
Carbohydrate	21g	Saturates	5g

Paper-thin Fruit Pies

Perfect for weight watchers, these crisp pastry cases, filled with fruit and glazed
with apricot jam, are best served hot with low-fat custard.

serves 4

1 eating apple	2 tbsp low-sugar apricot jam
1 ripe pear	1 tbsp unsweetened orange juice
2 tbsp lemon juice	1 tbsp finely chopped pistachio nuts
55 g/2 oz low-fat spread	2 tsp icing sugar, for dusting
225 g/8 oz filo pastry, thawed if frozen	low-fat custard, to serve

Method

❶ Preheat the oven to 200°C/400°F/ Gas Mark 6. Core and thinly slice the apple and pear and toss them in the lemon juice to prevent them discolouring.

❷ Melt the low-fat spread in a small saucepan over a low heat. Cut the sheets of pastry into 4 and cover with a clean, damp tea towel. Brush 4 non-stick, shallow tins, measuring 10 cm/4 inches across, with a little of the low-fat spread.

❸ Working on each pie separately, brush 4 sheets of pastry with low-fat spread. Press a small sheet of pastry into the base of 1 tin. Arrange the other sheets of pastry on top at slightly different angles. Repeat with the remaining sheets of

pastry to make another 3 pies. Arrange the apple and pear slices alternately in the centre of each pastry case and lightly crimp the edges of the pastry of each pie.

❹ Mix the jam and orange juice together until smooth and brush over the fruit. Bake in the preheated oven for 12–15 minutes. Sprinkle with the pistachio nuts, dust lightly with icing sugar and serve hot with low-fat custard.

Nutritional Information

Calories	158	Sugars	12g
Protein	2g	Fat	10g
Carbohydrate	14g	Saturates	2g

Mocha Swirl Mousse

A combination of feather-light yet richly moreish, these chocolate and coffee mousses are attractively presented in tall glasses.

serves 4

1 tbsp coffee and chicory essence

2 tsp cocoa powder, plus extra for dusting

1 tsp low-fat drinking chocolate powder

150 ml/5 fl oz low-fat crème fraîche, plus 4 tsp to serve

2 tsp powdered gelozone

2 tbsp boiling water

2 large egg whites

2 tbsp caster sugar

4 chocolate coffee beans, to serve

Method

❶ Place the coffee and chicory essence in a bowl, and the cocoa powder and drinking chocolate in a second bowl. Divide the crème fraîche between the 2 bowls and mix both well.

❷ Dissolve the gelozone in the boiling water and reserve. Whisk the egg whites and sugar in a clean, greasefree bowl until stiff and divide this evenly between the 2 mixtures.

❸ Divide the dissolved gelozone between the 2 mixtures and, using a large metal spoon, gently fold, until well mixed.

❹ Spoon small amounts of the 2 mousses alternately into 4 serving glasses and swirl together gently. Leave to chill for 1 hour, or until set.

❺ To serve, top each mousse with a teaspoonful of crème fraîche, a chocolate coffee bean and a light dusting of cocoa powder. Serve immediately.

Cook's tip

Gelozone, the vegetarian equivalent of gelatine, is available from most health food shops.

Nutritional Information

Calories	136	Sugars	10g
Protein	5g	Fat	8g
Carbohydrate	11g	Saturates	5g

Orange Syllabub

This is a zesty, creamy whip made from yogurt and milk with a hint of orange, served with light and luscious sweet sponge cakes.

serves 4

4 oranges

600 ml/1 pint low-fat natural yogurt

6 tbsp skimmed milk powder

4 tbsp caster sugar

1 tbsp grated orange rind

4 tbsp orange juice

2 egg whites

strips of orange zest, to decorate

Sponge hearts

2 eggs

6 tbsp caster sugar

40 g/1½ oz plain flour

40 g/1½ oz wholemeal flour

1 tbsp hot water

1 tsp icing sugar

Method

❶ Slice off the tops and bottoms of the oranges and remove the skin. Cut out the segments, removing the zest and the membranes. Divide the segments between 4 dessert glasses, then leave to chill.

❷ Mix the yogurt, milk powder, sugar, orange rind and juice together. Cover and chill for 1 hour. Whisk the egg whites until stiff, then fold into the yogurt mixture. Spoon onto the orange slices and chill for 1 hour. Decorate with orange zest.

❸ Preheat the oven to 220°C/425°F/ Gas Mark 7. To make the sponge hearts, line a 15 x 25-cm/6 x 10-inch baking tin with baking paper. Whisk the eggs and caster sugar together until thick and pale. Sift the flours, then fold into the eggs, adding the hot water at the same time. Pour into the prepared tin and bake in the preheated oven for 9–10 minutes, until golden on top and firm to the touch.

❹ Turn the sponge out on to a sheet of baking paper. Using a 5-cm/2-inch heart-shaped cutter, stamp out hearts from the sponge. Transfer to a wire rack to cool. Lightly dust with icing sugar before serving with the syllabub.

Nutritional Information

Calories 464

Protein 22g

Carbohydrate 89g

Sugars 74g

Fat 5g

Saturates 2g

Fruit & Nut Loaf

This loaf is like a fruit bread which may be served warm or cold, perhaps spread
with a little margarine or butter or topped with jam.

serves 4

225 g/8 oz white bread flour, plus extra
for dusting

½ tsp salt

1 tbsp margarine, plus extra for greasing

2 tbsp soft light brown sugar

50 g/1¾ oz no-soak dried apricots,
chopped

100 g/3½ oz sultanas

50 g/1¾ oz chopped hazelnuts

2 tsp easy-blend dried yeast

6 tbsp orange juice

6 tbsp low-fat natural yogurt

2 tbsp sieved apricot jam

Method

❶ Sift the flour and salt into a large bowl. Rub in the margarine and stir in the sugar, apricots, sultanas, nuts and yeast.

❷ Warm the orange juice in a saucepan but do not let it boil.

❸ Stir the warm orange juice into the flour mixture with the yogurt and bring the mixture together to form a dough.

❹ Knead the dough on a lightly floured work surface for 5 minutes, until smooth and elastic. Shape into a round and place on a lightly greased baking tray. Cover with a clean tea towel and leave to rise in a warm place until doubled in size.

❺ Preheat the oven to 220°C/425°F/ Gas Mark 7. Cook the loaf in the preheated oven for 35–40 minutes, until cooked through. Transfer to a wire rack and brush the cake with the apricot jam. Leave the cake to cool before serving.

Nutritional Information

Calories 531
Protein 12g
Carbohydrate 96g
Sugars 53g
Fat 14g
Saturates 2g

Carrot & Ginger Cake

This melt-in-the-mouth version of a favourite cake has a fraction
of the fat of the traditional cake.

serves 10

butter, for greasing

225 g/8 oz plain flour

1 tsp bicarbonate of soda

1 tsp baking powder

2 tsp ground ginger

½ tsp salt

175 g/6 oz light muscovado sugar

225 g/8 oz carrots, grated

2 pieces chopped stem ginger

25 g/1 oz grated fresh root ginger

55 g/2 oz seedless raisins

2 eggs, beaten

3 tbsp corn oil

juice of 1 orange

Icing

225 g/8 oz low-fat soft cheese

4 tbsp icing sugar

1 tsp vanilla essence

To decorate

grated carrot

finely chopped stem ginger

ground ginger

Method

❶ Preheat the oven to 180°C/350°F/ Gas Mark 4. Grease and line a 20-cm/ 8-inch round cake tin with baking paper.

❷ Sift the flour, bicarbonate of soda, baking powder, ground ginger and salt into a large bowl. Stir in the sugar, carrots, stem ginger, root ginger and raisins. Beat the eggs, oil and orange juice together, then pour into the bowl and mix well. Spoon into the tin and bake in the preheated oven for 1–1¼ hours, or until firm to the touch, or a skewer inserted into the centre of the cake comes out clean. Leave to cool completely in the tin.

❸ To make the icing, beat the cheese until soft. Sift in the icing sugar and add the vanilla essence. Mix well. Remove the cake from the tin and smooth the icing over the top. Decorate with grated carrot, stem ginger and ground ginger and serve.

Nutritional Information

Calories 249

Protein 7g

Carbohydrate 46g

Sugars 28g

Fat 6g

Saturates 1g

Recipe List

- Almond Trifles *82* • Baked Sea Bass *56* • Beef Teriyaki *46*

- Beef & Vegetable Soup *14* • Biryani with Onions *64* • Bruschetta *24*

- Carrot & Ginger Cake *94* • Charred Tuna Steaks *60* • Cheese & Chive Scones *26*

- Chicken & Almond Rissoles *20* • Fruit & Nut Loaf *92* • Fruity Muffins *78*

- Ginger Chicken & Corn *40* • Jerk Chicken *38* • Lemony Monkfish Skewers *58*

- Lentil & Ham Soup *12* • Minted Onion Bhajis *18* • Mixed Fruit Brûlées *84*

- Mocha Swirl Mousse *88* • Moroccan Salad *66* • Mushroom Cannelloni *68*

- Orange Syllabub *90* • Paper-thin Fruit Pies *86* • Pork Stroganoff *50*

- Potatoes with a Spicy Filling *28* • Red Mullet & Coconut Loaf *32*

- Rice & Tuna Peppers *30* • Savoury Hotpot *54* • Seafood Stir-fry *62*

- Skewered Spicy Tomato Chicken *42* • Spun Sugar Pears *72*

- Strawberry Meringues *80* • Summer Fruit Clafoutis *74* • Summer Fruit Salad *76*

- Sweet & Sour Drumsticks *22* • Tangy Pork Fillet *52* • Teppanyaki *44*

- Thai Red Chicken *36* • Tomato & Red Pepper Soup *10* • Wine-marinated Steaks *48*

- Yogurt & Spinach Soup *16*